Breaking Generational Curses

A New Beginning

Pernell Stoney

xulon
PRESS

Copyright © 2010 by Pernell Stoney

Breaking Generational Curses
A New Beginning
by Pernell Stoney

Printed in the United States of America

ISBN 9781615794577

All rights reserved solely by the author. The author guarantees all contents are original and do not infringe upon the legal rights of any other person or work. No part of this book may be reproduced in any form without the permission of the author. The views expressed in this book are not necessarily those of the publisher.

Unless otherwise indicated, Bible quotations are taken from The King James Version of the Bible.

www.xulonpress.com

ACKNOWLEDGMENTS

First, I give thanks to my Lord and Savior, Jesus Christ, who has given me the opportunity to share His Word and my testimony with you. I also give thanks to my wife, Hwason, a true friend and a woman of God, for still loving me after thirty years of bad and good times; to my daughter, Cherry, one of the sweetest people you ever could meet, always thinking of others first; and to my son, Steven, a man with strong family values. Even though I was not a part of his life growing up, as I should have been, he is always in my heart with a love that is unmatched. To my spiritual families: Minister James GiGi and DD Williams; Minister Johnny; Robin and Moses Williams. You guys are the greatest. God has given you a heart of love and caring and compassion; thanks for being there for us. Thanks to Dr. Michael and Brineta Mitchell, my pastors of Restoration Ministries International (RMI) Christian Fellowship in Augusta, Georgia, who have inspired me over the many years I have known them; Dr. Ron and Sue Rockwell, my pastors at Harvest Church, who not only teach the Word, but just as important, live the Word (love God; love people). Glendale, AZ, thanks for being our spiritual leaders in teaching us the Word of God and how to love each other. Apostle John Evans, thanks for your book, *It Is Not Your Fault, but It Is Your Time.* It shed a lot of light on this book. Again, thanks to all our friends; there are so many, I can't name them all. Just know that I love you with the love of God. Thanks for whatever part you played in my life. Remember, God loves you, and so do we.

DEDICATION

This book is dedicated to all those that may not know why they do the things they do, and how they can break that sin that so easily controls them, which is not their fault. It is time to make it right with God, ourselves, our families, our neighbors, and our friends.

TABLE OF CONTENTS

INTRODUCTION xi

CHAPTER 1   THE FALL OF MAN 13

CHAPTER 2   ALREADY AT WORK 25

CHAPTER 3   EMPTY VESSEL 29

CHAPTER 4   IT IS NOT YOUR FAULT, BUT IT'S TIME 33

CHAPTER 5   TRUE STORY 39

CHAPTER 6   BREAKING GENERATIONAL CURSES 52

CHAPTER 7	RELATIONSHIP	61
CHAPTER 8	A NEW BEGINNING	72
CHAPTER 9	NEW BIRTH	83
CHAPTER 10	PLACED INTO THE FAMILY OF GOD	90
CHAPTER 11	25 HEALING SCRIPTURES	103

INTRODUCTION

I know God wants you to break these curses that you have on your life, and to let you know that it is not your fault, but it is time to get equipped to do battle with this spiritual wickedness in high places. I will show you through the Scriptures that there are generational curses, and they have been passed down from our earthly fathers through generations. I will also show you how to break those curses through applying the Scriptures, the Word of God. There are many Scriptures that deal with this subject; the ones we will talk about are the ones I have studied. There are also generational blessings, and for those of you that are reaping them and know the Word of God should teach others. God's system is duplication, and when we learn the Word of God, we must teach others. Knowledge gained and kept for oneself benefits no one but oneself. Men and women of God are not selfish; this is why I am writing this book. I was taught on this subject, and it really changed my life. I know if it changed my life, it will change yours too. **So open your mind and heart, and let the Word of God minister to you.**

CHAPTER 1

THE FALL OF MAN

Let me start from the beginning so you will have an understanding and picture of our generational curses and how they came about. We first knew about curses in the book of Genesis starting in chapter 3 verse 14. I recommend you read the entire chapter. The serpent was the first creature cursed, because of what he did to EVE. The first human that was cursed was Eve; she was cursed with the pain of childbearing, and because Adam listened to his wife and ate from the forbidden tree, the curse was placed on the soil of the earth, that he would struggle all his life to make a living from the land. This was the beginning of the curse that was placed on man all because of his disobedience. Each generation since Adam has gotten worse and still is getting worse in the things that are forbidden. God gave our forefathers a way out of the curse by writing His commandments on a tablet so they could be seen and followed. In the book of Deuteronomy chapter 11 verses 26 through 28, **he said: "Behold, I set before you this day a blessing and a curse**; [27] **a blessing**, if ye obey the commandments of the LORD your God, which I command you this day: [28] and **a curse,** if ye will not obey the commandments of the LORD your God, but turn aside out of the way which I command you this day, to go after other gods, which ye have not known" (emphasis added). The commandments that were written down on the tablets are known as the laws of Moses. We are no longer under the law because God gave us another way out: He sent His only Son, that whosoever believeth in him should not perish, but have everlasting life. But our forefathers still did not heed the Word of the LORD, and the curse is still alive and destroying our families (we are still hanging on the tree). **Read Galatians 3:10-14**.

WHAT IS INIQUITY?

The bottom line: It is **SIN**. To break it down a little more, I have listed three things we do that fall under the umbrella of "sin."

1. Wickedness — We do things that are wickedly and morally bad without a second thought.

2. Sinfulness — We are a very sinful generation because of our relationship with the past, watching others. We start out with something small (most of us), and we keep adding to it, and before you know it, it gets easier and easier. It begins changing our mind/attitude, and we become what we are today through habit.

3. Guilt — When we have committed the sinful unrighteousness and wicked acts, we have that sense of guilt. Some of us do, and some don't.

All of us have or still fit into one or all of the above areas. This book will highlight some things you need to know in order for you to get your life back on track and right with God.

GENERATIONAL CURSE

A generational curse is a sin that is done over and over; in the Bible, it is known as iniquity (sin). Our earthly forefathers sinned repeatedly. To give an example, we can take a look at Exodus, the 32nd chapter, which talks about how the people worshiped a golden calf, drinking and dancing, much like we do today. You can also look at Genesis chapter 19, where the Lord destroyed Sodom and Gomorrah because of their evil and sinful ways. If you look at what they did back then and look at the way we are living today, you can see that generational curse still exists and has gotten stronger. In the King James Version of the Bible, the book of Jeremiah 31:29 states, "In those days they shall say no more, the fathers have eaten a sour grape, and the children's teeth are set on edge." I believe the writer is telling us that our forefathers lived a very sinful life, and it will have an effect on us if we don't get our act together. Just to name a few things that keep generational iniquity alive: cars, drugs, television, computers, fornication, love of money, same-sex marriage, lust, greed, physical and verbal abuse, and I can go on and on. When you begin to put them ahead of God and be disobedient to His Word, you are living the same lifestyle your forefathers did.

I want to show you something that will support what I am saying. Exodus 20:5-6: "Thou shalt not bow down thyself to them, nor serve them: for I the LORD thy God am a jealous God, visiting the INIQUITY of the fathers upon the children unto the third and fourth generation of them that hate me. [6] And shewing mercy unto thousands of them that love me, and keep my commandments" (emphasis added). The book of Lamentations 5:7 tells us, "Our fathers have sinned, and are not; and we have borne their iniquities" (being sinners of habit). This is telling us that our fathers have sinned repeatedly, and we are living in their footsteps. If you don't believe it, just take a look into your past and your father's, your grandparents', or a relative's past, and tell me what you see—some generational things, and I bet they are not all good. If we want to move forward in life and make changes, we must know where we came from and why we do the things we do. I would be willing to say 90 percent of you don't know your family history. Some of you don't want to know your family history, but I would tell you to take a look at it because you've got to start somewhere. If we don't stand up and fight, we will lose this battle on two fronts, spiritually and in the flesh. I believe these are Satan's targets, and he is doing a good job with this generation by taking the spirit first and having you work it out in the flesh.

THE TEN COMMANDMENTS

Before we get into the life-changing things, I must lay the foundation so you will see what the Holy Spirit is saying to you. The foundation is built on the Rock, and that Rock is Jesus Christ. He left two things for us. The first is the Ten Commandments, and we have totally thrown them out the window. And the devil is laughing at us. We were not taught, and we are not teaching our children. The first four commandments are relating to God; I will break them down for you.

1. "Thou shalt have no other gods before me." (Note: anything you put before God the Father is considered a god; i.e., money, sex, material things, even family.)

2. "Thou shalt not bow down thyself to them, nor serve them: for I the LORD thy God am a jealous

God, visiting the iniquity of the fathers upon the children unto the third and fourth generation of them that hate me."

3. "Thou shalt not take the name of the LORD thy God in vain; for the LORD will not hold him guiltless that taketh his name in vain."

4. Remember the Sabbath day, to keep it holy.

Let's break these four down a little more so you can get a better understanding.

1. Trust God only (Exodus 20:3).

2. Worship God only (Exodus 20:5-6)

3. Use God's name in ways that honor Him (20:7)

4. Rest on the Sabbath day and think about God (Exodus 20:8-11)

The next six are commandments relating to man's loving and respecting others.

5. "Honour thy father and thy mother: that thy days may be long upon the land which the LORD thy God giveth thee."

6. "Thou shalt not kill."

7. "Thou shalt not commit adultery."

8. "Thou shalt not steal."

9. "Thou shalt not bear false witness against thy neighbour."

10. "Thou shalt not covet thy neighbour's house, thou shalt not covet thy neighbour's wife, nor his manservant, nor his maidservant, nor his ox, nor his ass, nor any thing that is thy neighbour's."

Like the first four, I will break the last six down a little more to help you understand each one better.

5. Respect and obey your parents (Exodus 20:12). <u>This is the first commandment with a promise. If you do this, your days will be long upon this land.</u>

6. Protect and respect human life (Exodus 20:13). <u>We are not to be killing each other as we are doing today. There is a time to kill, and this is not the time. These are times for healing, and this is what we should be doing.</u>

7. Be true to your husband or wife (Exodus 20:14).

8. Do not take what belongs to others (Exodus 20:15).

9. Do not lie about others (Exodus 20:16).

10. Be satisfied with what you have (Exodus 20:17).

As you can see, we are not living according to the commandments that were laid out for us in the beginning. Our forefathers were disobedient, and we learn from them, and we are teaching our generation the ways of the world and not the Bible's way. With each generation, the iniquities and sins get worse, and it is time you know where they come from and why you do what you do.

Note: I am not saying the sinful life you are living comes from your family. It could come from the one you associate with. Let me remind you, everything we know and do comes as a learned response of someone telling us something, or something we have seen someone doing. Listed below are a few things our forefathers taught our fathers, and now we are teaching our children:

1. Sexual immorality—the TV, movies, nightclubs, music, and people association, to mention a few things.

2. Drunkenness—We saw our fathers drunk, so we drink, and our children see us drunk, and they do as we did (hmm).

3. Filthy language—This is something learned in the home and by association, and it is getting worse. Kids five and six years old are using filthy language; I wonder whom they learned it from (the curse must be broken).

4. Selfish ambition—thinking of self and no one else, making it to the top, not caring whom they step on.

5. Filthy outrage (anger)—no self-control when they can't get what they want. Does this sound like you?

6. Evil desires (lust)—wanting something or someone that belongs to someone else, and doing everything they can to get it.

7. Jealousy—can't stand to see someone else with something good or making something out of himself. Or wanting to be like the Browns.

8. Hatred—This is really a generational curse that is still strong today. How can we teach our children to hate a race of people that they don't know and when they have never seen all of them? But we are still doing it, and it is time to break that curse.

9. Envy—Instead of teaching our children to be all they can be, we teach them to be like someone else, creating envy in their hearts. Wake up, people. My God said He will supply all your need according to His riches in glory. Put your trust in Him and no one else.

10. Deceit—The nine things I mention above are all wrapped up in this one. This is the work of the devil that has controlled and is controlling our minds and is now moving on to our children through our generational curses.

The devil is being exposed in this book, and we are not going to be deceived anymore. We know he is at work, but it is our time to give him his pink slip; his service is no longer needed.

CHAPTER 2

ALREADY AT WORK

From the day we were born, the generational curses started. Let me take you back to the beginning, when the first man sinned (Adam) by being disobedient to what he was told not to do. Adam's disobedience started the generational curse. Every generation gets worse, and it will continue until you decide to do something about it. Already at work is the devil, Satan, Lucifer, who has many names and disguises, and who began his work that day in the garden. He has never stopped; just look around you. Look at your family tree, the things that are happening today. Our iniquities are getting worse. We were told over 2,000 years ago about this, and we are still being disobedient to His Word. Read

Genesis chapter 3 and 2 Thessalonians 1:7 (**already at work**). Our Lord and Savior "gave himself for us, that he might redeem (rescue) us from all iniquity (sins of habit), and purify unto himself a peculiar people, zealous of good works" (people with clean hearts and real enthusiasm for doing kind things for others) (Titus 2:14). In the book of Matthew chapter 24 verse 12, it tells us, "Because iniquity shall abound, the love of many shall wax cold." To explain this a little more, for you may not understand it, the Living Bible explains it like this: "Sin will be rampant everywhere and will cool the love of many." An example is marriages not lasting more than one to eight years, with people taking vows to love, to cherish, to have and to hold, till death do they part. The rate of divorce is sky high because of sin. There are young and old unwed mothers because of sin. There is killing, stealing, physical abuse, drug addition; I could go on and on. Iniquity has been imbedded in our spirit, body, and soul.

As you continue to read this book, I will tell you how to break this generational curse off your life, that you and your children may be saved. Our forefathers had some unclean spirits, and when they died, the spirits had nowhere to go until they found a place. That place for many of us is us. "Why me?" you say. Because you were fresh and clean, empty, and lacking in knowledge. The book of Matthew chapter 12 verses 43-45 tell me this is what happens to people that have a lack of knowledge: "When the unclean spirit is gone out of a man, he walketh through dry places, seeking rest, and findeth none. [44] Then he saith, I will return into my house from whence I came out; and when he is come, he findeth it empty, swept, and garnished. [45] Then goeth he, and taketh with himself seven other spirits more wicked than himself, and they enter in and dwell there: and the last state of that man is worse than the first. Even so shall it be also unto this wicked generation" **(already at work)**. Don't forget, Satan has been at this business a very long time and has many different tactics, but you need to know that he is defeated, and you learn that through the Word of God. We know the devil is already at work; now it is time we get to work reading God's Word, learning our rights and the power we have. In the Living Bible, 1 John 5:4 says, "For every child of God can obey him, defeating sin and evil pleasure by trusting Christ to help him." Remember, Satan only has the power we give him, and it is time we strip him of that power.

If we don't strip him and break this generational curse, it will transfer to your children. You can see the transfer has already taken place; we have kids eight years old shooting their parents, daughters getting pregnant at the age of twelve, children acting out in school, and their parents standing up for them. Kids as young as nine years old are plotting to massacre other school kids. Parents are letting them walk around with their pants hanging off their butts, which shows their underwear, and saying they are just being kids. Young girls are wearing miniskirts, high heels, and low-cut blouses with cleavage showing, and their parents smile and say they are just being cute (**Lord, help us**). Yes, I will say Satan is already at work. We as parents are blinded by the cares of this world and are not seeing what is really happening to us and our children. We must not fear the devil; we must stand on God's Word. In the book of 2 Timothy chapter 1 verse 7, it says, "For God hath not given us the spirit of fear; but of power, and of love, and of a sound mind." God has given us the power to overtake our enemies through faith and trust in Him, so examine yourself and your family history.

CHAPTER 3

EMPTY VESSEL

When you are living a worldly life, doing what the world does, your vessel is empty of the things of God. When it is empty, it gives Satan a place to stay, and when he takes up residence, he begins to work on ownership, taking control, telling you to do things that are not right and do them over and over until he takes over your soul. Let's take a look at Luke 22:3: "Then entered Satan into Judas surnamed Iscariot, being of the number of the twelve." Even though Judas walked with Christ, he was empty. He was a thief, all along stealing the money from the offering they received. When he betrayed Christ and realized what he had done was wrong, he then went out and hanged himself. Because of our empty vessels, we are allowing Satan and his demons to enter our bodies, all because of the cares of this world. The iniquities are getting worse and worse every generation.

Satan's primary goal is to deceive you and keep you busy with the things of this world. You must remember, he has been at this deceiving business a long time; the only way we can defeat him is to fill our mind, soul, and spirit with the things of God. Our iniquities have gotten so bad, they block our blessings. Here is what Jeremiah 5:25 tells us: "Your iniquities have turned away these things, and your sins have withholden good things from you." I hope you are seeing what I am trying to tell you: Our sinful lifestyle dictates our outcome. We wonder why we live from paycheck to paycheck. We wonder why our children act the way they do. We wonder why we are always sick. We wonder why no one likes us or we can't get along with others. I could go on and on, but the bottom line is we are living an iniquitous lifestyle. Jesus did not die on the cross for us to live this way, but until we come to the realization that we must change our lifestyle, iniquity will control our lives.

After you have read this book, you will never be the same; you will start looking at your generational line to see why you are the way you are. Let me point out that generational sin doesn't have to be the same type of sins. Sins are like a tree; it will start up with one branch and then begin to add on, and as generations pass, the tree gets bigger (sins). Sin is nothing but lies that Satan has whispered in your ear and told you are okay to do, and nothing will happen to you. Well, let me tell you, he is a liar, and the truth is not in him. When you stop believing those lies, your life will start to change. This is what the Word of God says in 2 Chronicles 7:14 (emphasis added): "If my people, which are called by my name, shall humble themselves, and **pray**, and **seek** my **face**, and turn from their wicked ways; then will I hear from heaven, and will forgive their sin, and will heal their land" (living in godly pleasures).

I was one of Satan's soldiers, listening to the whispers of his voice telling me to do things I knew were wrong, but he convinced me I could do them and get away with whatever I was doing (following in the footsteps of my earthly father). Well, let me tell you, listening to him cost me my first marriage, and almost my second marriage, thinking the things

I was doing I would get away with—staying out all night, drinking and gambling; smoking pot; neglecting my family. The sad thing about all the people I was hanging around was that most of them were not married, and none of them were saved. But the voice of Satan said it's okay, which was a big lie, and that is what he is good at. He knew I was an empty vessel with generational ties to my earthly father and did not have the knowledge of who I was in Christ. When you are empty, you are destroyed for the lack of knowledge. I know you've heard the saying that knowledge is power; well, that saying is so true. If you have the Word of God in you and do what He has put in you, using the Word in the way it is supposed to be used, you have unlimited power given to you from God the Father.

John 1:12 says: "But as many as received him, to them gave he POWER to become the SONs of God, even to them that believe on his name" (emphasis added). Note: With this type of power, Satan is already defeated, and he knows it, but we've got to show it, so we must stand up and let him know we have the victory.

CHAPTER 4

IT IS NOT YOUR FAULT, BUT IT'S TIME

In the book of Psalms 51:5, King James Version, it says, "Behold, I was shapen in iniquity; and in sin did my mother conceive me." Another translation, the Living Bible, says it like this: "But I was born a sinner, yes from the moment my mother conceived me." The reason you were born into sin is because of one man. Romans 5:12 says: "Wherefore, as by one man sin entered into the world, and death by sin; and so death passed upon all men, for that all have sinned." Now you see, it was not your fault, but it is your time to break this generational curse that has been placed upon you by those before you. Now that you know it was not your fault that you were born into sin, this is just the beginning of a spiritual battle that you will need the whole armor of God to win. For those of you that are still confused and don't believe you are carrying out generational curses, just do some research into your family history.

HOW DOES SATAN DO IT?

The devil is very cunning. He is slick. He is smart, and his number one entry point to your life is your weakness. He knows the flesh is weak by what we like and don't like. Think back for a moment on something you did and knew was wrong. Now this was not something that just happened. I would say to you it was in your mind for a few hours, if not for a few days or months. He will get you to lie, and after you have told the first lie, now you must tell another lie to cover up the first lie, and it just keeps on coming (iniquity/sin), and before you know it, it has destroyed your life and the ones who love you (family members and friends). His tactics could be anything that will keep you distracted from what God has for you if you follow His Son, Jesus.

Remember how he got to Eve in the Garden of Eden after God had told them not to eat from the tree that was in the middle of the garden, "neither shall you touch it, lest you die." The devil told her, "You will not die, but God knows when you eat it, your eyes will be opened and you will be like gods." He works the same way in your life today; all it takes is a smile or a wink of an eye or a smile by a man or a woman, and he will take that and put a thought in your mind. If you entertained that thought, he got you. These are tactics and acceptances that have been passed down for generation after generation. We must remember that Satan has no power; all he has are lies and deceit. He knows he is defeated, but you need to know he is defeated, and that is through the Word of our Lord and Savior, Jesus Christ.

Let me give you an example of what I saw Satan do to Christian men and women in the military. I will only talk about one place, Korea, but there are many other places where people act the same. I spent a lot of time in the country. I saw Christian men and women get in the country and see the fast and fun lifestyle, and Satan begin to whisper in their ears. He would tell them, "Nobody over here knows you. You are only here for a year, so let's have some fun. Nothing is going to happen." Well, again, the devil lied to them. Some of them got young girls pregnant;

some left the country and left their child (some of their fathers did the same things during the Korean war and after). Some of them are married, and some are single. Some ended up getting divorced. This divorce is not only from their wife; it is from God the Father. When other brothers in Christ try to reach out to them, they turn away and become angry. All of this is because of what Satan whispered in their ears. We must be strong in the Lord and in the power of His might. Our iniquities are really affecting our children, so please pay close attention to what I am going to write. This chart compared the top disciplinary problems of the '60s-'80s with the '90s through the present; this is what schoolteachers had to say.

1960s-80s — 1990s/2000

1. **Talking out of turn — Cursing the teacher**

2. **Chewing gum — Drug/alcohol abuse**

3. **Making noise — Making babies (pregnancy)**

4. **Running in the halls — Sex in the Restrooms**

5. Cutting in line — Cutting each other

6. Dress code infraction — Pants hanging off their butts

7. Littering — Robbery

8. Respect — Assault

9. Passing notes — Cell phone texting sex messages in class

10. Teachers counsel students about their behavior — Teachers running away with students, having sexual encounters

There are many more comparisons we could make that would let you know generations are getting worse. Demons are getting harder to resist because everyone else is doing it and having a good time, so why not us? It is a very bad attitude to think that way because some child, if not your own, is watching everything you do. This is how generational sin continues, and we must stop it now.

You ask yourself why kids are killing each other, why teen girls are getting pregnant, why drug and alcohol abuse is so strong in young people. Look at yourself and your fathers and mothers, grandfathers, grandmothers, great-grandparents, and so forth. Our family history could be filled with iniquity, and we are not doing anything about it. Before we can teach our children, we need to clean up our act and learn what the Word of God says. The Revised Standard Bible in the book of **Hosea 4:6 says: "My people are destroyed for lack of knowledge; because you have rejected knowledge, I reject you from being a priest to me. And since you have forgotten the law of your God, I also will forget your children."** You see, what we do and say affects our family, and when we don't do the Word of God ourselves, we can't teach our children; therefore, iniquity will abound from generation to generation. Don't forget, Satan is already at work, and his army is getting bigger and bigger every day. Please stop and take a look at what you are doing and make that change to receive God and His Word.

CHAPTER 5

TRUE STORY

A young man was born in a small southern town called Allendale with only one blinking light in the center of town. If you blinked, you had to look in the rearview mirror to see Main Street. He had four brothers and one sister. They told him his mother died when he was about six months old, and his father was nowhere to be found. His father left when his mother was pregnant with him. He was a pawn, and being the youngest, he was sent to live with relative after relative. In those days, it was very hard placing five kids in one family. They had to be split up among relatives. Finally, after about eight years of living with different relatives, he was sent to live with his grandmother. She was the sweetest person you could have ever met. She could not read or write, but she knew how to take care of you. When you were sick, she would make everything better. If you lived in her house, there were two things you had to do: work, and go to church, and every Sunday, he was in church. He really loved his grandmother, and he would do anything for her. By the time he started living with her, he had already picked up some bad habits hanging out with guys older than he was. He started smoking when he was nine years old, chasing young girls at the age of ten, and drinking and gambling at the age of thirteen. He was hiding all this from his grandmother. He had to be in the house by nine on school days, twelve on Fridays, and ten on Saturday nights. He made all of his curfew times because he knew at an early age to respect his grandmother and his elders. As he grew older, he stopped going to church, and his habits became stronger. The desires became addictive, and he began to lose control and get into trouble. He got married at the age of twenty-one, thinking married life could help him change. Well, married life did not change him, and things kept getting worse. After his wife became pregnant with their son, he said to himself that he would not leave like his father left him. He would teach his son sports, teach him how to ride a bike, do things with him his father did not do with him. Two years into his marriage, he was still smoking, drinking, chasing women, and gambling—the same things his father did—but he did not know this at the time all this was happening.

One day he came home from work, and his wife and son were gone. He found a note on the stove that read something like this: "You can have everything in the apartment. You will receive the divorce papers soon. P.S. Don't try to find me." At that moment, his heart dropped. He knew he had lost everything, so he started calling everyone he knew, even her mother; no one seemed to know where they were. He was living in a generational curse. The devil had lied to him all those years, but he was not aware of it. He really started drinking every day, staying at home, listening to sad, depressing music, hoping she would come back to him. About two weeks later, the phone rang, and it was his wife. She wanted to let him know where she was and that they were doing okay. He begged and pleaded with her to come back; he cried like a baby on the phone to no avail. He continued to drink even more, knowing she was not coming back to him. He blew all of his dreams of being with his son, seeing him grow, teaching and watching him play sports. One day he was home alone (smile). He was looking out the window, and he heard this voice say, "Stop feeling sorry for yourself, and begin to live." He started reading the Bible, not knowing what he was really reading, but he kept reading, and one day he decided to go into the Army, and he did. In April 1974, one week into basic training, he received his divorce papers. He was a free man on the outside, but hurting inside, losing all trust in women because of the hurt he was still feeling. Almost two years after his wife left him, he was still smoking, chasing women but not trusting, drinking, and reading his Bible. In 1974, he met the most beautiful woman he has ever seen, and they got married in 1977. He was still not a saved man, and he was still doing some of his bad habits, like smoking and gambling. His wife accepted the Lord as her Lord and Savior Jesus, but he was still doing his thing. Every Sunday his wife would beg him to go to church with her, but he would not. One weekend they decided to travel to Ohio to see her sister. At about 3 o'clock one morning, they, his wife and their four-year-old daughter, stopped at a rest stop for a couple of hours. After getting back on the road, driving about two hours, he smoked a joint while everyone was asleep. About thirty minutes later, he fell asleep driving and ran off the side of the road. He woke up and panicked, hitting the gas instead of the brake. They hit a ditch. The car flipped over and landed on the top, sliding down the highway on the opposite side and facing oncoming traffic. The front and back glass was completely gone. The car came to a stop. The top was completely crushed in. An eighteen-wheeler was heading for them, and by the grace of God, he noticed something in the road, and he slowed down. After seeing it was a car, he stopped, got out, and called for help. Because of the grace of God, the only injury was a small cut on his wife's knee. Everyone at the scene said they did not know anyone could have survived that kind of accident.

The car was totaled. He knew then someone was looking over him; he almost lost his whole family because he was living under a generational curse that had gotten worse in his generation from drinking to smoking dope, but he was not aware of the curse. In 1982, they went to Germany. There he became active in the church, but he was still smoking and drinking. The bad thing about that was he was doing these things with some of the brothers in the church.

One night he had a party at his apartment, and the young man got really drunk. His wife tried to get him to stop drinking and be nice. Well, he did not listen to her. Everyone wanted to go down to the pub, shoot some pool, and have a few more drinks. He said he was going to the pub. He was already drunk. His wife tried to stop him from going to no avail. Instead of walking to the pub, he decided to drive. After arriving at the pub, they began to drink more, and at about 3 A.M., he took his friend home that lived about fifteen minutes from his house. After getting to his apartment, they sat and talked for almost an hour. He was still drunk and should not have been driving. On his way back to his apartment, he hit a bump in the road, and his tapes fell on the floor. He tried to pick them up, and in doing so, he bent over and his foot pressed the accelerator. When he rose up, he was headed for a head-on collision with an apple tree. He panicked and turned the wheel too sharp at the speed he was going, and he drove the car to the side of a small cliff, head-on into another apple tree about twenty feet below. The car was totaled. He came out with just a small scratch on his shoulder. Looking back, he had an angel looking over and protecting him. At that time, he was more worried about what his wife was going to say when he told her his car was totaled and couldn't be fixed. She was very upset. She had begged him not to go out. After not getting hurt in the accident, his greatest fear was facing his wife. This was another sign for him to break the generational curse that was on his life. He did not know it was a curse because he did not know anything about his father's or his mother's lifestyle.

In 1986 in Augusta, GA, he attended the Living Word Christian Center. At that time, the pastor was George Lee; he prophesied over him and his wife, that they would do great things for the kingdom of God. At this time, he had stopped smoking and drinking, but still had a lustful eye. There was a young minister by the name of Michael Mitchell who preached one Sunday. The young man did not hear much of what was said; the young minister's action and fire in his eyes really lifted him up. Here was a young minister full of fire for God, and the young man wanted some of what the minister had, so his life began to change. But something was still not right. As years passed, he stayed in the Word, but was still having those feelings of smoking, drinking, chasing, and gambling. One day he heard T.D. Jakes speak about Peter and the lame man who was laid daily at the temple gate.

He had read this chapter before, but never saw what really happened to the man, what made him get up and walk. When he heard T.D. Jakes break it down, lights began to come on in the dark tunnels of his life. This is what caught his attention: Peter told the lame man to look on us, and the lame man gave heed unto them, expecting to receive something of them. It was not about money; it was about expecting and having faith. All these years, he was not really focused on God; his faith was weak, and he was not expecting anything except to satisfy himself. He began to dig deeper into his soul because something was still not clear, and that was why he was still doing things he did not want to do. A few years later, he was at his home church in Augusta, GA, Restoration Ministries International (RMI), with Dr. Michael and Bernita Mitchell. They had a Spiritual Warfare Conference, and Dr. I.V. Hilliard spoke on generational curses. He took very good notes, and he studied, and he studied, and he heard Dr. Mitchell, his pastor, speak on breaking generational curses. He took good notes, and he studied, and he studied. His dark tunnel was getting brighter and brighter.

EARTHLY FATHER

As he stated before, he never knew his father, only what he was told by his relatives, and they were not good things. He began to see the connection he had with his earthly father, who had a very serious generational curse on himself—the drinking, smoking, chasing women, lying, gambling, and a filthy mouth. He was told his father was a drunk, a cheat, and a gambler. He began to look back on his life, and he knew he was in a generational curse, and he had to do something about it before he would end up like his father, who died alone and broke. He really started getting into the Word of God, praying, fasting, and thanking Him every day for letting him see the error of his ways and thanking Him for his wife, who stuck by him, who prayed for him every day during his bad days, and who still prays for him today, and he thanks God for her. He gave up his old running friends that could not see why he wanted to stop partying. He started making new friends, becoming a member of a Bible study group like the Men of the Morning, Calm, Men of Valor in Okinawa and Korea, and attending Spiritual retreats that talked about Jesus, our Lord and Savior. He had friends like Pastor John

Bivins (JR), who kept him in the right frame of mind just by being in his company, and also beat him on the golf course and praised God at the same time; and Ministers Johnny and James Williams, who talk about Jesus Christ daily, planting the seed of faith, righteousness, and love. Today that young man in the story is spreading the Word of God to everyone. God has even given him words to write.

The young man in this story is I. Through all the bad things I did and was doing while still in church, God knew my heart, and the more of the Word I received, it convicted my spirit. Learning what my generational curse was gave me a target to shoot and kill, and I began to change my wicked and evil way. If God can change me, He can change you too, but you must have a willing heart. Also remember, you can't have a future without a past; look into your past so you can find your future. We all were born into a generational curse, and it only took one man to create this mess, so don't think what you say or do doesn't matter, because it does; every generation a curse gets worse. Just look at me; I did twice the things my father did, and if you don't change, you will be worse than your father or the bad people you hang out with. Some of you are already there. If you don't think there is a generational curse, just look in the prisons; you will see fathers, sons, and even grandsons, even mothers, daughters, and granddaughters, all there because of one person's act. The sin you do is against God, and when you do the crime, you must do the time. Remember, when you are living in iniquity, you are not only hurting yourself, but everyone that cares for you, especially the children. **"They that are left of you shall pine [waste] away in their iniquity in your enemies' lands; and also in the iniquities of their fathers shall they pine away" (Leviticus 26:39).** Are you going to waste away and go to hell because of what your father did, or are you going to stand up like a man of God and fight for your freedom through the Spirit? As apostle John Evans would say, **"IT IS NOT YOUR FAULT, BUT IT IS YOUR TIME."** It is your time to take a stand and take back what the devil has stolen from you.

In the next few chapters, I will help you get started on breaking that generational curse by sharing Scriptures and testimonies. Before we go to the next chapter, let me ask you a question: When we go to the doctor, why do they always ask us our family history? Did your mother or your father have this or that? To answer the question, it is a generational thing, because if they had it, you are more likely to have it or will get it—makes you think, hmm! The devil also knows it is a generational thing, and if our father or mother was one of his soldiers, guess what? He will try to recruit you too, all because of that familiar spirit he had or has with your parents. Take a look at the word "familiar" (family). One of Webster's meanings for the word "familiar" is having good knowledge of something. The iniquities that your fathers and mothers did he knows, and his job is to keep all family members in his army. Brothers and sisters, this is not a battle you can win in the flesh; this is a spiritual war that must be fought in the Spirit.

"For though we walk in the flesh, we do not war after the flesh: (For the weapons of our warfare are not carnal, but mighty through God to the pulling down of strong holds)" (2 Corinthians 10:3-4). Well, we can no longer blame our fathers; I know it was not our fault, but it is our time. In the book of **Jeremiah in the 31st chapter, the 30th verse** tells us, "Every one shall die for his own iniquity: every man that eateth the sour grape, his teeth shall be set on edge." We have been living in our parents' iniquities all these years; it is time to break this generational curse. We are responsible for our lives, and it is time to make it right through the grace of our Lord and Savior, Jesus Christ. This is a life-and-death decision you will make. If you are living in your father's iniquity, you have already made a decision. Some of you know that you made bad decisions, and some of you did not know you were living in your parents' iniquities. Take a look at your past and present actions, and you will know it is time to change. There is still eternal life for all of us. In the next few chapters, I will try to give you help in making that life-changing decision.

CHAPTER 6

BREAKING GENERATIONAL CURSES

Following are nine keys to breaking a generational curse.

(Spiritual Warfare)

<u>(It's not your fault, but it is your time.)</u>

1. SEEK
2. FAITH
3. TRUST
4. PRAYER
5. COMMITMENT
6. STUDY

7. TEACH
8. RELATIONSHIP
9. FAMILY

There are more keys to breaking a curse, but these are the ones I have been led to write about in this book. Please pay close attention to what you are about to read because how you receive them and apply them to your life is very important. The first step we need to take is to **seek** Him (Matthew 6:33) and then have faith, faith that there is a God and He sent His only Son to save us, and that His Son died on the cross for you and me. You see, faith is the key to receiving the promises. Hebrews 11:1 says, "Now **faith** is the substance of things hoped for, the evidence of things not seen." Just having faith alone is not enough because we need something with that faith. You need to have works with your faith in order for it to manifest in your life, so read James 2:17. You may ask yourself, How can I get faith? Let me answer that for you. Faith comes by hearing the Word of God (Romans 10:17). Hebrews 11:6 tells us, "Without faith it is impossible to please him [God]: for he that cometh to God must believe that he is, and that he is a rewarder of them that diligently seek him."

The work you need to do is seek the kingdom of God first; with your faith and all His righteousness, believe what His Word says. Then you will be able to have victory in your spiritual battles (Matthew 6:33). It's refreshing when you are dirty after a long day of work and you go home and take a shower or a bath. When it is complete, don't you feel good? That's what turning your life over to God can do for you—give you freshness above all freshness. Like the old commercial used to say, "Try it; you may like it," I'll say to you, you will like it (read Acts 3:19). When accepting Christ, you must be willing to have your heart clean because out of the heart come the issues of life. In the book of Psalms chapter 51, after David was confronted by Nathan the prophet after he had gone into Bathsheba, in verse 2, David said, "Wash me throughly from mine iniquity, and cleanse me from my sin." We must ask God to give us strength, that we may cleanse our iniquity and sins. In verse 10, he asks God to create in him a clean heart and renew a right spirit within him. We must be willing to be completely changed from the inside out, and with a clean heart comes a right spirit. This is not going to be a walk in the park; you will be in a battle, a real war that is fought in the spirit. This war is no different from any other war because they all start in the spirit realm and act out in the flesh. What we are going to do is fight it where it began, in the spirit. We all know when you go to battle, you must have on your battle gear. Our battle gear is the Word of God, our loins grit about with truth, the breastplate of righteousness, our feet shod with the preparation of the gospel, taking the shield of faith (ye shall be able to quench all the fiery darts of the wicked, anything that the devil may throw at you), taking the helmet of salvation and the sword of the spirit, which is the Word of God. This is why we must stay in the Word, so we can be ready in season and out. Read Ephesians chapter 4 verses 23-29; also read Ephesians chapter 6 verses 10-17.

We must learn how to pray with a pure heart because God knows our heart. Out of the heart come the issues of life. We must be serious when we pray and not say things just to be saying them, repeating the same things over and over. When you do that, that lets God know you don't believe He heard you the first time or that you don't believe He will answer your prayer. This is why **faith** and **trust** are so important in the Word of God—if we don't have them, we will not receive anything from God. So please spend time praying; it does not matter whether you are on your knees, standing, or lying down. In the book of Luke chapter 18 verse 1, it says that "men ought always to pray, and not to faint" (not give up). First Thessalonians 5:17 tells us to "pray without ceasing." **Prayer** is a key to breaking that generational curse. Proverbs 16:3 tells us to **commit.** Be real, be committed, and stop making excuses as to why you can't come to church or read your Bible, why you can't come to Sunday school, and why you can't come to Bible study. If it is one of your hobbies or something you like to do, I bet you make time to do it. Now that you are learning what it will take to break that generational curse on your life, stop making excuses, and be committed to yourself and to God. Second Timothy 2:15 tells us, "**Study** to shew thyself approved unto God, a workman that needeth not to be ashamed, rightly dividing the word of truth."

If we can study our homework from school, college, the university, and other things that are related to our daily lives, we can study God's Word too. If you don't remember anything else, remember this: **What does it profit a man to gain the whole world and lose his soul?** When we learn the Word of God, we must **teach** our children the Word; we must start a new generation. The only way to do that is to teach our children the Word of God; this is what my Bible tells me to do. In the book of Deuteronomy 6:6-7, it says, "And these words, which I command thee this day, shall be in thine heart: [7] And thou shalt teach them diligently unto thy children, and shalt talk of them when thou sittest in thine house, and when thou walkest by the way, and when thou liest down, and when thou risest up." I know some of our fathers may not have taught us like it tells us in the book of Deuteronomy, and it is not our fault, but it is our time. It is time for us to get it right by learning and teaching. Whatever your generational curse may be, you are on the road to Damascus; the spirit of God is working in you to complete the change. When I think of where I came from—faced with death, drugs, drinking, women, gambling, lying, and stealing—and where I am today, it could have only been by the grace of God that I am here. I know some of you may have done worse or less; it is not about how much you did or how little you did. It is all about the decision you will make today. I made a decision a few years ago to make Jesus Christ my Lord and Savior, and today He is using me and my testimony to let you know He will do the same for you. All you have to do is take that first step. If you have friends that are doing the same things you are, it is time you cut them loose or bring them with you. If they are not willing to change and accept Christ as their Lord and Savior, you need to drop them like a hot potato. Why? Because they will only talk you out of accepting Christ. When you get strong in the Word, your actions and your testimony will have a much greater effect on them and others that are waiting for your testimony. God not only has a plan for you; He also has a blessing with your name on it. The Word of God is the light of the world; the more you put in you, the brighter you will look and the straighter you will walk. In the book of Joshua in the 24th chapter, verse 15 tells us to <u>choose</u> whom we are going to serve. This is a decision that must come from the heart.

It must start on the inside, and it will work its way to the outside. You can make the decision on your own, but you will have help through fellowship, group Bible study, and new friends that are living for the Lord. Another very important ingredient in breaking generational curses is establishing a **relationship**.

Everything we do in this world today has a root of relationship. Examples include if you are married, if you are single, your girlfriend or your boyfriend, your car, your clothes, your food, your favorite actor, your computer, your TV, sports, daytime and nighttime soaps ... I could go on and on with the things we have a relationship with, and all of them will pass away because they are temporary things placed here to distract us from having a real, everlasting relationship. That relationship is with Jesus Christ. In order for us to get that relationship, we must do as it states in the book of Matthew 6:33: **"But seek ye first the kingdom of God, and his righteousness; and all these things shall be added unto you"** (emphasis added). Know him, just like you got to know the things I mentioned above; you took time for them, and they will pass away. The relationship you establish with Him will never pass away; it is a true relationship that loves you in spite of everything. The bottom line is the closer you get to God, the easier it is to break that generational curse on you and your family. **Family** is also important in seeking a relationship with Christ. If you are the only one in your family seeking Christ and that new beginning, it will be hard, but you must stay focused on what you want to achieve, and that is a relationship with Christ, to change your present state or lifestyle. Hooking up with a spiritual family—i.e., a pastor, or men or women fellowship groups—is a very good means of keeping one focused. If your family members are already saved, they should be pillars of strength in helping you with studying and praying, giving you all the support that you need to help put the negative past where it belongs. Brothers and sisters, I am a witness that having a relationship with my Lord and Savior, Jesus Christ, has really changed my life. I am aware of my generational curse that had plagued me all my life, and now I know how to fight it by trusting and believing in God's Word.

Another lesson I learned is you can't fight something that you don't know you have because you don't know what weapon to use in order to get the victory. Well, studying the Word of God will give two things that assure you victory. It's the relationship with Christ, and with that relationship, you will receive the weapons of warfare, and with the weapons of warfare, you are always ready for war. Later in this book, I will give a few things the enemy will try to use in his spiritual battle.

CHAPTER 7

RELATIONSHIP

In this chapter, we will talk about relationship because it is the main key to one changing his or her attitude, lifestyle, and the way he or she speaks. What does the word "relationship" mean, the state or fact of being RELATED, connection by BLOOD, or marriage? The state of affairs among people or dealing with one another; as you can see, relationship is part of us. In anything we do, we have some type of connection, whether with an object or with someone. We are related to Christ through His blood. He died on the cross for us so we could be saved from sin, and that is the ultimate relationship. We all have a connection to our Lord and Savior, Jesus, for He is the beginning and the ending. If we don't have a relationship with Him, we are lost, and our foundation is built on sinking sand. Let's look at some of the relationships that are built on sinking sand that the devil has diverted for his pleasure. The following are going on without a real relationship and a solid foundation of Christ.

<u>Sex</u>—The act is out of control, with people sleeping with anybody and everybody, man with man, woman with woman. This is not the way God intended for sex to be done, but the media will have you think it is okay to live this type of lifestyle.

<u>Money</u>—The relationship we have with money we have put before God, not knowing, or forgetting, that it is **<u>God who gives us "power to get wealth, that he may establish his covenant which he sware unto thy fathers, as it is this DAY"</u>** (Deuteronomy 8:18, emphasis added). The Word tells us in the book of **<u>1 Timothy 6:10, "For the love of money is the root of all evil: which while some coveted after, they have erred from the faith, and pierced themselves through with many sorrows."</u>** Just take a look at the things that are happening today over oil, and land, and people are robbing, killing each other for money, and, yes, it is a generational thing.

Drugs—God gave man the ability to develop different types of drugs for medical use, and Satan has poisoned the minds of men to convert what God gave them for good and now use it for evil, and with each generation it gets worse.

Alcohol has also become a stumbling block in the lives of many, creating sorrow and pain, because its usage leaves a mark on the next generation.

There are many types of relationships. I just named a few that I can relate to our generational line that you may not be aware of that could change your life from death to eternal life. Everything has a beginning, and there will be an ending; before your end comes, I want to make you aware of the generational curse that may be on you.

If you don't think you have a generational curse, don't leave one for someone to follow unless it is the way of the Lord. Anything or person you gravitate toward more than another, you have a relationship with. If you have a lustful eye (sex), you will begin to cheat, or already are cheating, on the person you are with. If you have a greedy spirit (money), you have already cheated, or are about to begin to cheat, someone out of something. If you like to go to nightclubs and party, you have a relationship with one of the following: drugs, alcohol, or sex. These are all generational curses that need to be broken. Friends, what kind do you have? What direction are they leading you? I say that because you are doing one or the other, leading or following. In today's world, we let our environment change us because we don't want to offend anyone by telling them we are Christians and we believe in Christ. What we are doing is following in the generational ways that cause us to sin. If you are weak and easily led astray, check your generational line because you have taken on their ways. **<u>First Corinthians 15:33 tells us, "Be not deceived: evil communications corrupt good manners."</u>** Break generational curses and study the Word; build up faith and confidence, and build a strong foundation, one that can't be broken. I can't stress enough how important it is to establish a relationship with my Lord and Savior, Jesus Christ. Without a spiritual relationship with the Father, we are dead spiritually, causing this generation to be worse than **Sodom** and **Gomorrah,** full of sin and iniquity. Let us go back to the beginning of all this so I can show you a few things. In the book of Genesis, the 3rd chapter, starting at verse 1, it says: "Now the serpent was more subtil [difficult to detect, skillful, ingenious, clever, capable of making fine distinctions] than any beast of the field which the LORD God had made. And he said unto the woman [Eve], Yea, hath God said, Ye shall not eat of every tree of the garden? (now he has her thinking, just like he has you thinking today when you know what you are doing is wrong) ² And the woman said unto the serpent, We may eat of the fruit of the trees of the garden: ³ But of the fruit of the tree which is in the midst of the garden, God hath said, Ye shall not eat of it, neither shall ye touch it, lest ye die."

You see, she is telling the serpent what God told them. Now can you see the generation relation we have because God has told us through His Word what to do and not to do? ⁴ And the serpent said unto the woman, Ye shall not surely die [this was the first lie that was told to man, and man believed it, and look at what has happened to man]: ⁵ For God doth know that in the day ye eat thereof, then your eyes shall be opened, and ye shall be as gods, knowing good and evil." I know it was not our fault that the woman ate the fruit and that was the fall of man. Well, it is our time to break this curse off of us and get back that relationship that was lost. The Word of God is being politicized by men of God, and believers are saying what people want to hear and not what the Bible says. Believe it or not, our lives are based on relationships; everything we do, we have some type of relationship with it. As I stated above in the definition of "relationship," one aspect was connection, being connected to someone or something. Here are some things we are connected to that drive us from having a closer relationship with the Father and our Lord and Savior, Jesus Christ: Money—we lie, cheat, steal, even kill for it; cars—we even wash them on Sunday when we should be at church; TV—we watch so much of it, we don't have time to study the Word of God (the Bible); computers and video games—we spend even more time playing them, thus neglecting to study the Word; we neglect family and have no time to attend church; clothes—we worry about what we do have, spending money on things we don't need, not paying our tithes and offerings to God (**Malachi 3:8**). Again, there are many things we have a relationship with that distract us from a real relationship with Christ. We can send our children to school and help them study to pass a test, but we won't sit down with them to study His Word or even let them see us studying the Word to be blessed and know the truth. I will say to you, **"Seek ye first the kingdom of God,**

and his righteousness; and all these things shall be added unto you" (Matthew 6:33). All these by themselves are not bad, but Satan has blinded the eyes of so many of us, that we are living in reverse. Trying to have relationships with all these things first and putting God last, calling on Him only when you get in trouble or are sick, is the type of relationship that is just like our forefathers (generational things), only it is getting worse. It is becoming a modern-day Sodom and Gomorrah.

CHILDREN

Our children are the future, and they are very impressionable; just take a look at us. How easy it is for someone to impress us with the big gold chains around our necks, the pants hanging off our butts, the language we use, the music we listen to, the big, fancy car, the big houses with a mortgage payment that we can't make, the Gucci and LV purse that cost four or five hundred dollars with nothing inside of them. Don't misunderstand me; those things are good to have, and God wants us to have good things. It is what we do with them when we get them that is important. We are making a big impression on our kids, and you ask why they are killing each other over things, drugs, money, and sex. They have a relationship with us; we are their teachers, leading them down that wide street of destruction that only leads to death. **Ephesians 5:6** says, "Let no man deceive you with vain words: for because of these things cometh the wrath of God upon the children of **disobedience**." Please stop and take a good look at what we are doing to ourselves and our children. God is not pleased with us about what we are doing. What I am about to write next has been on my mind for quite some time, as I've been trying to figure out how to put it on paper. The Holy Spirit has broken it down to me like this: First, let me say, sin and iniquity are running wild in today's world. There are a few states that are pushing hard for same-sex marriages, and there is one that has already allowed that to happen. Now, let's go back to the beginning, when God created the earth. He created man, and from man he created woman. **Genesis 1:27-28 says, "So God created man in his own image, in the image of God created he him; male and female created he them. 28 And God blessed them, and God said unto them, Be fruitful, and multiply, and replenish the earth, and subdue it: and have dominion over the fish**

of the sea, and over the fowl of the air, and over every living thing that moveth upon the earth."

There are a few things I would like to point out. First, it was a man and a woman and not a man and a man, or a woman and a woman. The next point I would like to bring out: God told them to be fruitful and multiply. If I understand what the Word of God is saying, it is telling me that same-sex humans should not get married. This is not what God intended for man; two of the same sex can't be fruitful and multiply. What man is doing is against the laws of God. I believe this is another generational curse, and over the years, it has gotten worse, and it will continue to if we don't take a stand on God's Word. That should and will be broken with the studying of the Word of God. Please don't say, "I was born like this," because God did not and will not create homosexuals and lesbians. I believe this is something someone learned from a relationship as a child and as an adult. We should not hate the person, but we should hate the act and pray for the person because this is what is happening: **"For we wrestle not against flesh and blood, but against principalities, against powers, against the rulers of the darkness of this world, against spiritual wickedness in high** places" **(Ephesians 6:12).** As you can see, it is not the person; it is an act of the devil, and he is defeated through prayer, so we need to get on our knees day and night. <u>**Isaiah 5:20 says, "Woe unto them that call evil good, and good evil; that put darkness for light, and light for darkness; that put bitter for sweet, and sweet for bitter!"**</u> We have let generational curses overpower our spiritual values. We have exploited the poor and call it the lottery. We have rewarded laziness and call it welfare. We have killed our unborn and call it choice. We have shot abortionists and call it justifiable. We have neglected to discipline our children and call it building self-esteem. We have abused power and call it politics. We have coveted our neighbor's possessions and call it ambition. We have polluted the air with profanity and pornography and call it freedom of expression. We have let men marry men, and women marry women, and call it equal rights.

Please take a look around you, and for those of you that can think back twenty, thirty years ago, you can see how the generational curses are getting worse. If we don't do something about it now, it will continue to get worse with each generation. Fathers need to stand up and be real fathers, teaching their children the Word of God, leading by example and not by teaching the things of the world. Remember, everyone has a relationship with someone or something, and with that relationship, the person learns habits from the person that is doing the leading. My question for you: **What type of leader are you? Do you know that your family generational curse is on you?**

Nugget 1: When you have a relationship with the Son, all things are possible (Luke 18:27).

Nugget 2: You can do all things (Philippians 4:13).

Nugget 3: You are able (2 Corinthians 9:8).

Nugget 4: You can cast your cares on Him (1 Peter 5:7).

CHAPTER 8

A NEW BEGINNING

Below are nuggets you can carry with you in the new beginning:

Nugget 1: He will give you rest (Matthew 11:28-30).

Nugget 2: He loves you (John 3:16).

Nugget 3: His grace is sufficient (2 Corinthians 12:9).

Nugget 4: He will supply all your needs (Philippians 4:19).

Nugget 5: He will direct your steps (Proverbs 3:5-6).

Nugget 6: He has not given you the spirit of fear (2 Timothy 1:7).

Nugget 7: He has given everyone a measure of faith (Romans 12:3) as you trust Him.

And the last nugget, #8, is to always remember, He will never leave you or forsake you (Hebrews 13:5).

In order for us to start something new, we must acknowledge the old things and the things that did not work. We must also understand why they did not work. I believe this is one of the reasons we fall back into the same iniquities day after day. When you are in a war or before you go to war, you must study to know the different types of tactics the enemy can and will use in order to try and defeat you. Below is a list of things you must be aware of at all times because the enemy will surely use them to his advantage.

Note: There are five things you must protect daily:

1. Your eyes (what you look at and how you look at it). **First John 2:16** says, "For all that is in the world, the lust of the flesh, and the lust of the **EYES,** and the pride of life, is not of the Father, but is of the world" (emphasis added). **Proverbs 10:10** says, "He that winketh with the **EYE** causeth sorrow: but a prating fool shall fall" (emphasis added). To break it down a little more, when you look at something or someone with a lustful eye, it is a tactic of the enemy that seems right, but in the end, it leads to spiritual death. When we look at the opposite sex, we wink and smile with lustful thoughts in our minds, all because we yield to the tactics of the enemy. Again, I believe this is something that has been passed down through the generations and is getting worse.

2. Your mouth (watch what you say). **Psalm 39:1** says, "I said, I will take heed to my ways, that I sin not with my tongue: I will keep my mouth with a bridle, while the wicked is before me." And **Ephesians 4:29** says, "Let no corrupt communication proceed out of your mouth, but that which is good to the use of edifying, that it may minister grace unto the hearers."

We must always watch what we say. There is an old saying that goes like this: Sticks and stones may break my bones, but words don't bother me." I know some of you have heard that before, and you know that is not true. Words are very powerful; they can lift you up or tear you down. The devil has influenced you to say things that were very hurtful to someone, and he is still on the move doing the same old things. Protect your mouth with the Word of God; put it in your heart, and it will guide you.

3. Your ears (be very careful what and whom you listen to). **Second Timothy 4:3-4** says, "For the time will come when they will not endure sound doctrine; but after their own lusts shall they heap to themselves teachers, having itching ears; [4] and they shall turn away their ears from the truth, and shall be turned unto fables." I will tell you to study the Word for yourself, so you will know the true Word when you hear it. Protect your ears with the Word of God.

Note: The music we listen to and let our children listen to that is filled with profanity and sexual lyrics is accepted in this devilish society, and we wonder why people act the way they do. We have

conformed to the world's way, and it is time to break this one life at a time, starting with you.

4. Your flesh (what and how you feel can lead down the wrong path). **Matthew 26:41** says, "Watch and pray, that ye enter not into temptation: the spirit indeed is willing, but the flesh is weak." Even with the Word in us, our flesh will rise up on us. This is why we must pray constantly. That means pray without ceasing (1 Thessalonians 5:17). Controlling the flesh is done through God's Word. Try it; I am sure you will feel the change.

5. Your heart (if you don't protect your heart, it will kill you). **Matthew 15:18-19** says, "But those things which proceed out of the mouth come forth from the heart; and they defile the man. [If you don't know these things, verse 19 will tell you.] [19] For out of the heart proceed evil thoughts, murders, adulteries, fornications, thefts, false witness, blasphemies." (Now you see why it is so important to protect the heart with the Word of God. The evil can be replaced with God's Word, but you've got to study His Word daily.)

Note: With sins that never come to the knowledge of the truth, **it is not our fault, but it is our time. Read 2 Timothy 3:1-7.**

BE AWARE OF THE 5 D's OF SATAN

1. Disguise. Satan has many ways and things to come at you with. If you are a person that has an eye for the opposite sex, and you are a married man, he will disguise himself as the most beautiful female or handsome male you have ever seen, just to cause you to sin. If you are broke and need money, he will disguise the honest way to get money, causing you to steal, even kill someone, for the money. He is a master of disguise. I could go on and on about his disguises, but you get the picture. The Word of God will bring those disguises to light.

2. Distort. He will try to confuse you by not letting you receive the correct information by bringing a multitude of things to your mind at the same time you are trying to hear or read the Word of God. Confusion is his game. He knows if he can keep you distorted and confused, he can recruit you into his army, so be wise as to his tactics.

3. Divert. His mission is to change your course to get you off the narrow road of eternal life. He wants you to get on the wide road of destruction, the road that seems good but is full of iniquity and sin. If it is not lining up with the Word of God, it is a diversion of Satan. Let me give you an example of diverting: It is payday, and it is time to pay your tithes and give your offerings. There is a brand new iPod, Xbox, cell phone, or Wii game on the market, and you have wanted one for quite some time. The more you thought about the item, the easier it was for Satan to divert you from paying your tithes and offerings. He will tell you that you can make it up the next paycheck. This is how he operates: He will help you bring that thought to reality. The only way you will know it is a diversion of the devil is by knowing the Word of God and following it.

4. Deny. He will have you believe the Word of God is untrue, just as he did to Eve in the garden. You can read the story in Genesis chapter 3. He will harden your heart; you will refuse to believe the Word of God. The Word tells us that God's people are destroyed for lack of knowledge and the rejection of knowledge (read Hosea 4:6). When you study the Word (2 Timothy 2:15), you can overcome those tricks of the devil.

5. Discredit. He will destroy your reputation with lies and disbeliefs; he will start rumors, and he will cause you to lose trust in what God can and will do for you. He will whisper anything into your ear to make you see and hear in a spiritual manner, causing you to act out in the flesh and hurt people that love you. That is why it is so important to put on the armor of God (Ephesians 6:10-18).

THE 7 C's OF SPIRITUAL SUCCESS

There are many ways to achieve success spiritually. I am just going to give you what the Holy Spirit told me to put in this book for you. We all want to be successful in life, not knowing that there are two types of success. My question to you is, What type of success do you want, fleshly success or spiritual success?

1. Christ is the first C in having any kind of Spiritual success. **Galatians 2:20** says, "I am crucified with Christ: nevertheless I live; yet not I, but Christ liveth in me: and the life which I now live in the flesh I live by the faith of the Son of God, who loved me, and gave himself for me. (Read Matthew 6:33.)

2. Character—You must be a person with moral qualities; others can distinguish one person or group from another. **Titus 2:14** says, "Who gave himself for us, that he might redeem us from all iniquity, and purify unto himself a peculiar people, zealous of good works."

3. Charity (love)—You must have a heart full of charity, and it must be in spite of the same type of love God gave to us. In the book of 1 Timothy 1:5, it says, "Now the end of the commandment is charity out of a pure heart, and of a good conscience, and of faith unfeigned."

4. Commitment—You must be committed to God through His Word, not backsliding when things get a little rough. **Psalm 37:5** says, "Commit thy way unto the LORD; trust also in him; and he shall bring it to pass."

5. Consistency—Anything we do in life, if we want to be good at it, we must be consistent in doing it. The Word of God is no different when it comes to consistency. In **2 Timothy 2:15**, it says, "Study to shew thyself approved unto God, a workman that needeth not to be ashamed, rightly dividing the word of truth. *Consistently studying the Word shows commitment, and in the end, you will be rewarded for your work.

6. Confidence—You must have faith in the Word of God and that He has given you the ability to be spiritually successful. In the book of Hebrews 3:6, it says, "But Christ as a son over his own house; whose house are we, if we hold fast the confidence and the rejoicing of the hope firm unto the end."

7. Concentration—You must stay focused, keeping your eyes on your goal to be obedient to the Word of God. It tells us that in the book of Joshua 1:8: "This book of the law shall not depart out of thy mouth; but thou shalt meditate therein day and night, that thou mayest observe to do according to all that is written therein: for then thou shalt make thy way prosperous, and then thou shalt have good success."

So, my brothers and sisters, the bottom line is this: Jesus Christ defeated the curse by HIS faithfulness to every word that proceeded out of the mouth of HIS FATHER, even unto death on the cross and HIS subsequent resurrection. We don't have to live in the curses of our earthly fathers. As I stated before, it is not our fault, but it is our time. Take a stand, and ask God to create a clean heart and renew a right spirit within you. The angels in heaven are rejoicing because you have accepted Christ into your life, and a change is taking place in the spirit realm.

CHAPTER 9

NEW BIRTH (Born Again)

Study to show yourself approved.

Fill in the blank with the correct chapter and verse.

1. "But seek ye first the kingdom of God, and his righteousness; and all these things shall be added unto you." _____.

2. "Therefore if any man be in Christ, he is a new creature: old things are passed away; behold, all things are become new." _____.

3. "That if thou shalt confess with thy mouth the Lord Jesus, and shalt believe in thine heart that God hath raised him from the dead, thou shalt be saved. For with the heart man believeth unto righteousness; and with the mouth confession is made unto salvation." _____.

4. "But as many as received him, to them gave he power to become the sons of God, even to them that believe on his name. Which were born, not of blood, nor of the will of the flesh, nor of the will of man, but of God." _____.

5. "All that the Father giveth me shall come to me; and him that cometh to me I will in no wise cast out." _____.

6. "Verily, verily, I say unto you, He that heareth my word, and believeth on him that sent me, hath everlasting life, and shall not come into condemnation; but is passed from death unto life." _____.

7. "Repent ye therefore, and be converted, that your sins may be blotted out, when the times of

Breaking Generational Curses

refreshing shall come from the presence of the Lord." _____.

8. "For by grace are ye saved through faith; and that not of yourselves: it is the gift of God: Not of works, lest any man should boast." _____.

9. "Verily, verily, I say unto thee, Except a man be born of water and of the Spirit, he cannot enter into the kingdom of God." _____.

10. "If we confess our sins, he is faithful and just to forgive us our sins, and to cleanse us from all unrighteousness." _____.

11. "It is the spirit that quickeneth; the flesh profiteth nothing: the words that I speak unto you, they are spirit, and they are life. **But there are some of you that believe not**." _____.

NOTE: When you study and meditate on God's Word, it begins to speak to you. All you need to do is open your mind, your heart, and your ears; you will hear that soft voice giving you instructions. If you are obedient to what you hear, you

will begin to see the change in your life, breaking that generational curse that has stopped you from getting your blessings, all that God has for you.

12. "Now ye are clean through the word which I have spoken unto you. Abide in me, and I in you. As the branch cannot bear fruit of itself, except it abide in the vine; no more can ye, except ye abide in me."_____.

13. "Being born again, not of corruptible seed, but of incorruptible, by the word of God, which liveth and abideth for ever."_____.

14. When you become born again, you belong to Him, and this is what He says about you: "But ye are a chosen generation, a royal priesthood, an holy nation, a peculiar people; that ye should shew forth the praises of him who hath called you out of darkness into his marvellous light."_____.

NOTE: When you ask for forgiveness and accept Christ as your Lord and Savior, you enter the war zone where spiritual battles are fought. Whenever we go to war, we must be battle-ready, and our

weapon is the Word of God. These battles are spiritual and are fought in the spirit realm (in our mind), causing us to act them out in the flesh. Learning God's Word will enable you to block those fiery darts that the enemy will throw at you. When we do the following, we are ready for battle:

We must put on the new man.

15. "[23] And be renewed in the spirit of your mind; [24] And that ye put on the new man, which after God is created in righteousness and true holiness. [25] Wherefore putting away lying, speak every man truth with his neighbour: for we are members of one another. [26] Be YE ANGRY, AND SIN NOT: let not the sun go down upon your wrath: [27] Neither give place to the devil. [28] Let him that stole steal no more: but rather let him labour, working with his hands the thing which is good, that he may have to give to him that needeth. [29] Let no corrupt communication proceed out of your mouth, but that which is good to the use of edifying, that it may minister grace unto the hearers."_____.

Getting dressed for battle:

16. "Finally, my brethren, be strong in the Lord, and in the power of his might. Put on the whole armour of God, that ye may be able to stand against the wiles of the devil. For we wrestle not against flesh and blood, but against principalities, against powers, against the rulers of the darkness of this world, against spiritual wickedness in high places. Wherefore take unto you the **whole armour of God**, that ye may be able to withstand in the evil day, and having done all, to stand. Stand therefore, having your **loins girt** about with **truth**, and having on the **breastplate of righteousness;** And your **feet** shod with the preparation of the **gospel** of peace; Above all, taking the **shield of faith**, wherewith ye shall be able to quench all the fiery darts of the wicked. And take the **helmet of salvation**, and the **sword of the Spirit**, which is the **word** of God." _____.

As you can see, God's super shopping center has everything you need to break those generational curses; we just need to change where we shop. Please take a real look around you, and you can see each generation is getting worse. I beg you

to look into your family history and the company you keep, and you will have a better understanding as to why you do the things you do. If you let God touch you, He will change you; He will only act on your request, and He is waiting on you. Please remember this: "Christ's death on the cross included a sacrifice for all our sins, past, present, and future. Every sin that you will ever commit has already been paid for. All of our sins were future when Christ died two thousand years ago. There is no sin that you will ever commit that has not already been included in Christ's death." —Erwin W. Lutzer (1941–)

PRAYER

GRACIOUS AND HEAVENLY FATHER, I PRAY THE BLOOD OF YOUR DEAR SON, JESUS, UPON EVERYONE WHO ACCEPTS YOUR SON, JESUS, AS THE LORD AND SAVIOR OF THEIR LIVES. I PRAY THE MESSAGE IN THIS BOOK WILL ENLIGHTEN THE HEARTS AND MINDS OF EVERYONE THAT READS IT. FATHER, I PRAY THIS IN THY SON, JESUS' NAME, AMEN.

CHAPTER 10

PLACED INTO THE FAMILY OF GOD

We all were placed into the family of God because we are His offspring that He created, for He is the Creator. "For in him we live, and move, and have our being; as certain also of your own poets have said, for we are also his offspring. Forasmuch then as we are the offspring of God, we ought not to think that the Godhead is like unto gold, or silver, or stone, graven by art and man's device" (**Acts 17:28-29**). We were not brought into God's family because of what we did; it was only because He loves us. This relationship, however, is not sufficient to offset the penalty of sin because all persons are sinners separated from God. "**For all have sinned, and come**

short of the glory of God" (Romans 3:23). For a sinful person to become a child of God, a miraculous transformation must take place. **The Bible refers to this change as being born again. "Jesus answered and said unto him, Verily, verily, I say unto thee, Except a man be born again, he cannot see the kingdom of God" (John 3:3). Note:** We must break this generational curse that is on our lives starting with ourselves so we can teach our children and keep them in the family of God. When an individual places his faith in Christ as Savior, he is born again into a new, spiritual, family relationship with God. He gains God as Father and other Christians as brothers and sisters. In the family of God, there is UNITY. **"There is one body, and one Spirit, even as ye are called in one hope of your calling; one Lord, one faith, one baptism, one God and Father of all, who is above all, and through all, and in you all" (Ephesians 4:4-6).** It is significant to note the term "brotherly love," which Christians are commanded to have for each other. **["Let brotherly love continue" (Hebrews 13:1).]** Christians are children of God by spiritual birth; they are adopted as well. In the book of **Ephesians 1:5**, it tells us, **"Having predestinated us unto the adoption of children by Jesus Christ**

to himself, according to the good pleasure of his will."

Note: When the Father sent His only begotten Son to die on the cross for us, the door was opened for us to come back into the family of God; what are you waiting for? When you come into the family of God, you are no longer under the devil's control. You are not in bondage anymore. You are a free son possessing all the rights and privileges of sonship. One of these benefits is the right to call God Abba, an affectionate term meaning *Father*. This marvelous relationship carries responsibilities with it, as well as privileges. Everyone who has the hope of having his sonship perfected someday is presently purifying his own life. Since he bears the family relationship to God, he must also exhibit the family character.

THE FRUITS OF THE SPIRIT (Character of the Father)

The first fruit is LOVE. It seeks the highest good of others.

LOVE is not based on emotions or feelings. It is a decision to be committed to the well-being of others without any conditions or circumstances.

a) John 3:16

b) Jesus said: As the Father has loved me, so have I loved you. Now remain in My love (John 15:9).

c) Jesus also said: My command is this: Love each other as I have loved you. Greater love has no man than this, that he lay down his life for his friends. You are My friends if you do what I command (John 15:12-14).

d) Look at 1 John 4:7-12.

JOY: Gladness not based on circumstances.

Joy is more than happiness; it is not based on financial success, good health, or popularity. By believing in God, obeying His will, receiving His forgiveness, participating in fellowship with other believers, ministering to others, and sharing the gospel, believers will experience joy.

a) Look at John 17:13 (Christ praying for His disciples).

b) Look at John 16:22-24 (this is talking about the death and resurrection).

c) Look at 1 Peter 1:8-9 (trials for the present).

PEACE: Contentment, unity between people.

Peace is a state of assurance, a lack of fear, and a sense of contentment. It is fellowship, harmony, and unity between individuals. Peace is freedom from worry, disturbance, and oppressive thoughts.

a) Let us turn to Isaiah 9:6.

b) Now if you are not convinced, turn to Luke 2:11.

c) Let us, therefore, follow after the things that make for <u>PEACE</u>, and things wherewith one may edify another. Read Philippians 4:6-7.

<u>PATIENCE: We must be slow to speak and slow to anger.</u>

Patience is slowness in avenging wrongs. It is the quality of restraint that prevents believers from speaking or acting hastily in the face of disagreement, opposition, or persecution. Patience is bearing pain or problems without complaining.

a) Read 1 Timothy 1:15-16 (we are made in God's image; we must have patience like Him toward our brothers and sisters and others).

b) The book of Proverbs 14:29 tells us a patient man has great understanding, but a quick-tempered man displays folly. (Folly—a lack of good sense or foresight.)

c) A hot-tempered man stirs up dissension, but a PATIENT man calms a quarrel (Proverbs 15:18).

d) We are to warn those that are idle, encourage the timid, help the weak by being PATIENT with everyone (1 Thessalonians 5:14).

KINDNESS: Kind is merciful, sweet, and tender.

Kindness is an eagerness to put others at ease. It is a sweet and attractive temperament that shows friendly regard.

a) Read Titus 3:4-5 (by washing away our sins and giving us the indwelling of the Holy Spirit). A kindhearted woman gains respect, but a ruthless man gains only wealth.

b) A kindhearted man benefits himself, but a cruel man brings trouble on himself (Proverbs 11:16-17).

c) Let us turn to Jeremiah 9:23-24.

GOODNESS: Good is generous and open-hearted.

GOODNESS is the selfless desire to be open-hearted and generous to others above what they deserve.

a) Turn with me to Ephesians 5:8-10.

b) "Let us not be weary in well doing: for in due season we shall reap, if we faint not. As we have therefore opportunity, let us do good unto all men, especially unto them who are of the household of faith" (Galatians 6:9-10).

FAITHFULNESS: Faithful is dependable, loyal, and full of trust.

Faithfulness is firm devotion to God, loyalty to friends, and dependability to carry out responsibilities. Faith is the conviction that even now God is working and acting on one's behalf.

a) Let love and faithfulness never leave you; bind them around your neck write them on the tables of your heart (Proverbs 3:3).

b) Read Matthew 23:23 (we may tithe, but we must not forget to be faithful in other things in our Christian walk).

c) Be faithful, even to the point of death, and I will give you the crown of life (Revelation 2:10b).

GENTLENESS: Gentle is humble, calm, nonthreatening.

Gentleness is a humble, nonthreatening demeanor that derives from a position of strength and authority, and is useful in calming another's anger.

GENTLENESS is not a quality that is weak and passive.

a) Read Matthew 11:28-30 (be gentle and humble—treat people like you would want to be treated).

b) Proverbs 15:1 (A soft answer turns away wrath: but grievous words stir up anger.

c) Question: Do you want someone to come to you in love and with a gentle spirit? (1 Corinthians 2:21).

d) Read Philippians 4:4-5 (some translations will say, let your gentleness be evident to all).

e) 1 Peter 3:15, Living Bible: "Quietly trust yourself to Christ your Lord and if anybody asks why you believe as you do, be ready to tell him, and do it in a gentle and respectful way."

SELF-CONTROL: Behaving well.

Self-control is restraint of one's emotions and desires, and harmony with the will of God. Having self-control is doing God's will, not living for oneself.

a) On the night Jesus was betrayed, he knelt down and prayed. "Father, if you are willing, take this

cup from me; yet not my will, but yours be done" (Luke 22:42).

When he was accused, he never retaliated. He showed remarkable self-control. A man without self-control is as defenseless as a city with broken-down walls (Proverbs 25:28, Living Bible).

A fool gives full vent to his anger, but a wise man keeps himself under control (Proverbs 29:11). Read Titus 2:11-12.

Finally, my brothers and sisters, "submit yourselves therefore to God. Resist the devil, and he will flee from you. Draw nigh to God, and he will draw nigh to you. Cleanse your hands, ye sinners; and purify your hearts, ye double minded" (James 4:7-8).

I am going to leave you with something to think about:

1. Do you have life insurance?

2. What is the name of your insurance company?

3. Is your premium paid weekly, biweekly, or monthly?

4. What kind of life insurance do you have?

5. Let me name a few companies; maybe you can claim one of them:

a) New York Life

b) Prudential

c) Mutual of Omaha

d) AAA

e) USAA

There are many that I have not mentioned. I think I have mentioned enough for you to get what I am going to bring to your attention. The insurance companies I mentioned are not the companies you need for life insurance. The companies you have are death companies because when you die, someone will collect some money or benefit from your death.

If you want real insurance, you need to be insured by the KINGDOM of GOD through His Son, Jesus Christ. He provides real life insurance that no person or company can provide.

The president is pushing for everyone to have insurance, I am also pushing for everyone to have life insurance—life insurance with our Lord and Savior, Jesus Christ. All it takes is for you to say, "I accept Jesus as my Lord and Savior," and then begin to read His Word and fellowship with other believers. Now you will begin to see and feel the change in your life. The change will come from the inside. Praise Him and give Him thanks every day, and your premium is paid daily. You can keep your death insurance; it will leave your loved ones an inheritance, which we all are to leave our children. The most important thing is how to live a good Christian life, having a relationship with the Father.

CHAPTER 11

25 HEALING SCRIPTURES

There are many Scriptures that deal with healing, and most of us don't know what God says about healing. When we get sick, the first thing we do is call the doctor or go to the emergency room. I am not saying not to do that, but I am saying the first doctor you should be calling is DR. JESUS. He will prepare the way for you so you can receive your healing. It is not always physical; there are many forms of sickness. Whatever you have, God can make it go away, but you've got to trust Him with what He says in His Word. When you are feeling down and out, turn to these Scriptures, read and meditate on them, put them in your heart, and let God refresh your spirit. Our faith must be with action because His Word says faith without works is dead (**James 2:17**). If you truly believe in your heart what you have read and are about to read, God has manifested and will manifest healing in your life.

1. "Heal me, O LORD, and I shall be healed; save me, and I shall be saved: for thou art my praise" **(JEREMIAH 17:14).**

2. "And ye shall serve the LORD your God, and he shall bless thy bread, and thy water; and I will take sickness away from the midst of thee" **(EXODUS 23:25).**

3. "And said, If thou wilt diligently hearken to the voice of the LORD thy God, and wilt do that which is right in his sight, and wilt give ear to his commandments, and keep all his statutes, I will put none of these diseases upon thee, which I have brought upon the Egyptians: for I am the LORD that healeth thee" **(EXODUS 15:26).**

4. "Many are the afflictions of the righteous: but the LORD delivereth him out of them all" **(PSALM 34:19).**

5. "He sent his word, and healed them, and delivered them from their destructions. Oh that men would praise the LORD for his goodness, and for his wonderful works to the children of men!" **(PSALM 107:20-21).**

6. "When the even was come, they brought unto him many that were possessed with devils: and he cast out the spirits with his word, and healed all that were sick: that it might be fulfilled which was spoken by Esaias the prophet, saying, Himself took our infirmities, and bare our sicknesses" **(MATTHEW 8:16-17).**

7. "Come unto me, all ye that labour and are heavy laden, and I will give you rest. Take my yoke upon you, and learn of me; for I am meek and lowly in heart: and ye shall find rest unto your souls. For my yoke is easy, and my burden is light" **(MATTHEW 11:28-30).**

8. "What shall we then say to these things? If GOD be for us, who can be against us? He that spared not his own Son, but delivered him up for us all, how shall he not with him also freely give us all things" **(ROMANS 8:31-32).**

9. "Thou wilt keep him in perfect peace, whose mind is stayed on thee: because he trusteth in thee" **(ISAIAH 26:3).**

10. "UNTO thee, O LORD, do I lift up my soul. O my GOD, I trust in thee: let me not be ashamed, let not mine enemies triumph over me. Yea, let none that wait on thee be ashamed: let them be ashamed which transgress without cause. Shew me thy ways, O LORD; teach me thy paths. Lead me in thy truth, and teach me: for thou art the GOD of my salvation; on thee do I wait all the day" **(PSALM 25:1-5).**

11. "Beloved, I wish above all things that thou mayest prosper and be in health, even as thy soul prospereth" **(3 JOHN 1:2).**

NOTE: When you are going through things, no matter what they are, you must have faith; you must have hope and believe what He said in His Word is true. Then you will begin to see the fullness of His love.

12. "Now faith is the substance of things hoped for, the evidence of things not seen" **(HEBREWS 11:1).**

13. "But without faith it is impossible to please him: for he that cometh to GOD must believe that he is, and that he is a rewarder of them that diligently seek him" **(HEBREWS 11:6).**

14. "So then faith cometh by hearing, and hearing by the word of GOD" **(ROMANS 10:17).**

15. "Humble yourselves therefore under the mighty hand of GOD, that he may exalt you in due time. Casting all your care upon him; for he careth for you" **(1 PETER 5:6-7).**

16. "Be careful for nothing; but in every thing by prayer and supplication with thanksgiving let your requests be made known unto GOD. And the peace of GOD, which passeth all understanding, shall keep your hearts and minds through Christ Jesus" **(PHILIPPIANS 4:6-7).**

17. "Trust in the LORD with all thine heart; and lean not unto thine own understanding. In all thy ways acknowledge him, and he shall direct thy paths. Be not wise in thine own eyes: fear the LORD, and depart from evil. It shall be health to thy navel, and marrow to thy bones" **(PROVERBS 3:5-8).**

18. "If my people, which are called by my name, shall humble themselves, and pray, and seek my face, and turn from their wicked ways; then will I hear from heaven, and will forgive their sin, and will heal their land" **(2 CHRONICLES 7:14).**

19. "There shall no evil befall thee, neither shall any plague come nigh thy dwelling. For he shall give his angels charge over thee, to keep thee in all thy ways. They shall bear thee up in their hands, lest thou dash thy foot against a stone" **(PSALM 91:10-12).**

20. "Who his own self bear our sins in his own body on the tree, that we, being dead to sins, should live unto righteousness: by whose stripes ye were healed" **(1 PETER 2:24).**

21. "He healeth the broken in heart, and bindeth up their wounds" **(PSALM 147:3).**

22. "O LORD my GOD, I cried unto thee, and thou hast healed me" **(PSALM 30:2).**

23. "Fear thou not; for I am with thee: be not dismayed; for I am thy GOD: I will strengthen thee; yea, I will help thee; yea, I will uphold thee with the right hand of my righteousness" **(ISAIAH 41:10).**

24. "And Peter said unto him, Aeneas, Jesus Christ maketh thee whole: arise, and make thy bed. And he arose immediately" **(ACTS 9:34).**

25. "But my GOD shall supply all your need according to his riches in glory by Christ Jesus" **(PHILIPPIANS 4:19).**

GET WISDOM! GET UNDERSTANDING!

1. To be almost saved is to be totally lost.

2. WARNING: Exposure to the Son can prevent burning.

3. Watch your step carefully! Everyone else does!

4. We don't change the message; the message changes us.

5. Wisdom has two parts: 1) having a lot to say, and 2) not saying it.

6. Worry is the darkroom in which "negatives" are developed.

7. The work will wait while you look at the rainbow, but the rainbow won't wait while you do the work.

8. Pray is a four-letter word that you can use anywhere.

9. Nothing ruins the truth like stretching it.

10. The will of God will never take you where the grace of God will not protect you.

SUMMARY

There are many Scriptures in the Bible that talk about healing; I just put a few in this book in the hope they will minister to you as you read this book. You don't have to be physically sick to be healed; there is mental sickness also that needs healing. I believe every family fits into one of the two categories of physical or mental sickness, which I also believe comes from that generational curse. Break that curse, and the sickness will go away; that is what the Word of God tells me. **Each one of us will have to pay for our own sins and iniquities, and Christ has already paid for them, so why pay for them again? Stop and take a good look at your lifestyle, and ask yourself, Is this what I am supposed to be doing with my life? I can tell you it is not about the big house, the expensive car, the high-paying job, your big-screen TV, your computer, or any tangible thing. I will tell you it is all about Jesus Christ and having a relationship with Him; when you seek and receive Him first, all those other things will come.**

We must not let the world's moral values and standards take charge of our thinking. Instead, we must let the Holy Spirit direct our thinking, by the renewing of our minds. Then we are able to understand what God's will is for our lives. The Word of God says it best: "**And be not conformed to this world: but be ye transformed by the renewing of your mind, that ye may prove what is that good, and acceptable, and perfect, will of God" (Romans 12:2).**

Please study God's Word and open your mind and have faith that He is who He says He is. He has made a way for us. All we need to do is get back on the right path. Joshua 1:8 also gives us a guide to stay on the right path and be successful in life. THANKS.

I truly thank you for taking the time to read this message. If you have already heard this message before, please let someone else read it. The knowledge you have gained is not only for you, so please pass it on because a testimony of what God has done for us ministers to others makes the angels in heaven rejoice. It was not your fault, but it is your time to set your life in order. May the grace of God continue to be upon you as you break that generational curse and start a new beginning.

LISTED BELOW ARE A FEW POEMS I WROTE JUST FOR YOU

I HAVE SHOWN YOU THE WAY

I have shown you the way; all I ask is for you to stay.
You live like it is a stage; My love for you has no age
You have a leading role, so please give Me your love to hold
Horses and cows love hay; do not ever forget My love for you is here to stay.
Follow Me, and I will show you the way.

A SPECIAL FRIEND

You are my friend; you are like an angel from heaven; you are someone
Special, someone who would give his last dime, someone who gives
His time, someone who will go for long walks just to listen to a friend talk
Someone who would cry when I cry, and someone who would smile when I

Smile. You are a special friend; you are a lifeline that I need in my life all the
time. **Thanks for being my special Friend**.

MY FATHER

As far back as I can think, you were always there for me.
After all, a father's love is from heaven above, and it covers us all.
The things you do for us all keep you walking tall.
Here are my words to you; thanks, dad, for I love you too.
Every day you teach us to love each other, for we are sisters and brothers.
Remembering your love and support; this is why I am sending you this note.
Father of the year, you have my vote. **My Father**.

JUST BECAUSE OF WHO YOU ARE

Because of who you are, I will give you my all
Because of who you are, I will always be here when you call

Because of who you are, I will always love you no matter if near or far
Because of who you are, I will always love you just because.

WALK BY FAITH

I walk by faith because of His grace
I feel joy when I am in His place
His love is strong; He walks with me
all day long. I walk by faith, and it is at His place
He gives me insight and the spirit to fight; I walk by
Faith and not by sight.

A LETTER FROM A FRIEND TO A FRIEND

Dear Friend,

How are you today? I just had to send you a note to tell you how much I love you and care about you. I saw you talking with your friends yesterday, and I waited all day, hoping you would want to talk to me also. As evening drew near, I gave you a sunset to close your day and a cool breeze to rest you.

I waited; you never did call on me. Oh, yes, it hurts, but I still love you because I am your friend. I watched you fall asleep last night. How I longed to touch your brow and comfort you. Instead, I spilled moonlight upon your pillow and your face. Again, wanting to rush to you so that we could talk.

I have so many gifts for you. This morning you awakened late, and you rushed about your work with no thought of me, and my tears joined the rain. Today you looked so sad and so alone. I wanted to touch you and let you know I was near. But I didn't. It makes my heart ache to see you so sad. I understand what it is like when your friends hurt you and let you down. My friends have done that to me many times; I will love you no matter what, because I understand. Oh, if you would only believe how much I love you. If you would stop long enough to listen to me when I speak to you.

I speak to you in the blue sky and in the green grass. I whisper my love for you in the leaves on the trees. I breathe my love in the scent of the flowers. I shout it to you in the mountain streams. I sing to you in the bird's song. I clothe you with warmth of the sunlight and give you perfume to scent the air you breathe. My love for you is deeper than the oceans and bigger than the biggest want or need you could ever have. Oh, if you only knew how much I want to talk with you. We could spend eternity together in heaven. I do know how difficult it is living in your world ... I really do know.

I want you to meet my Father. He can and will help you. My Father is like that, you know. Please come and talk to me anytime; I am your friend. It is your decision. I have chosen you, and will wait ... because I do love you.

Your Friend,
Jesus